The Toytown rescue

Story by Jenny Giles
Illustrations by Richard Hoit

Here comes

the Toytown helicopter.

Toytown Garage

"The bus is down

in the grass!"

said the helicopter

to the tow truck.

"Come on!"

Toytown Garage

5

Away went the tow truck.

Away went the helicopter.

"I can not see the bus," said the tow truck to the helicopter.

9

"I can see the bus,"

said the helicopter.

"Come down to the big tree."

The tow truck went down
to the big tree.
"I can see the bus!"
said the tow truck.

"Good," said the helicopter.

"Oh, I am happy to see you," said the bus.

"Come on," said the tow truck.

15

"Come home to the garage."